BUILD YOUR OWN
SPECTACULAR
MODEL SPACECRAFT

Rob Ives

CONTENTS

PREPARE FOR LIFTOFF	4	SAFETY FIRST!	6

SPECTACULAR MODEL SPACECRAFT	8	BLOWPIPE SPACE SHUTTLE	20
STOMP ROCKET	10	ORIGAMI MARS LANDER	22
MOON LANDER	14	BALANCING UFO	24
ROCKET CAROUSEL	16	AMAZING SPACECRAFT	28
MARS ROVER	18	PREPARING FOR LAUNCH	30

GLOSSARY AND INDEX	32

Copyright © 2024 Hungry Tomato Ltd

First published in 2024 by Hungry Tomato Ltd
F15, Old Bakery Studios, Blewetts Wharf, Malpas Road, Truro, Cornwall,
TR1 1QH, UK.

No part of this publication may be reproduced, stored in a retrieval system, or transmitted in any form or by any means, electronic, mechanical, photocopying, recording, or otherwise, without prior written permission of the copyright owner. A CIP catalogue record for this book is available from the British Library.

ISBN 9781916598850

Printed in China

Discover more at
www.hungrytomato.com

PREPARE FOR LIFTOFF

Try your hand at building amazing space-themed models! Using smart and simple engineering principles, you can make a whole collection of out-of-this-world crafts that hover, fly, move, and show the wonders of our universe and beyond!

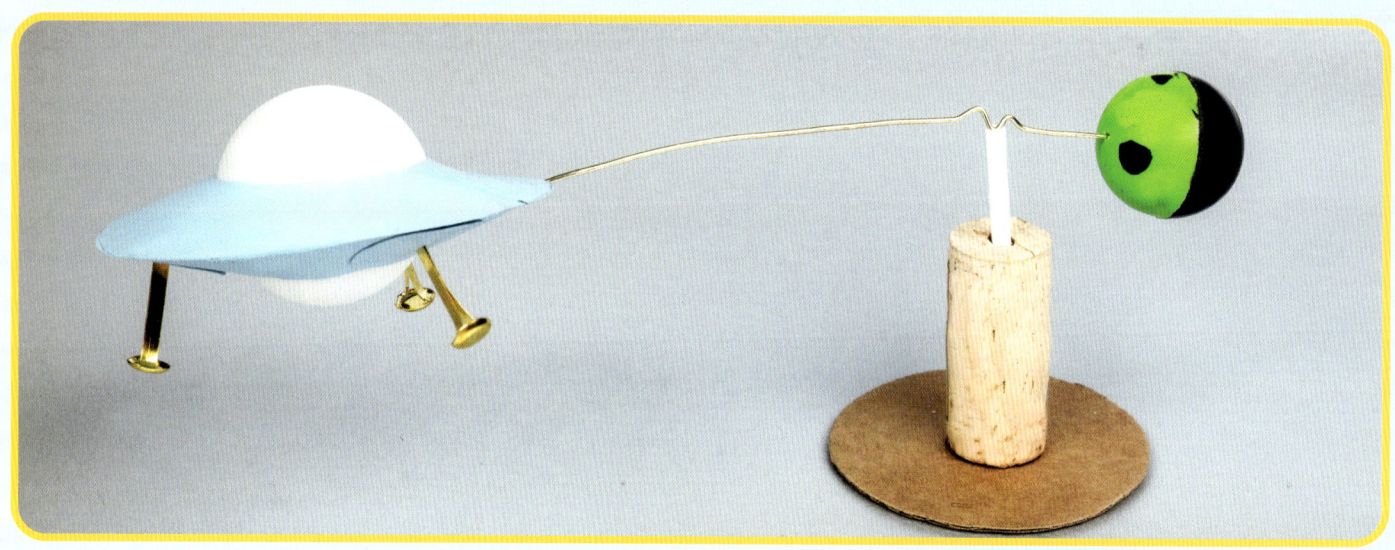

THIS BOOK IS INTERACTIVE!

Some of the projects in this book come with templates to help you cut pieces to the right shape and size. Use a smartphone to scan the QR code at the beginning of the project to access a downloadable template that you can print out.

You will find QR codes at the end of some projects, too. These will direct you to videos of the moving models in action!

You can also find all templates and videos at:
www.hungrytomato.com/model-spacecraft

PREPARE FOR LIFTOFF

TOP TIPS

- Before you start any project, read the step-by-steps all the way through to get an idea of what you are aiming for. The pictures show what the steps tell you.

- When printing templates, check that your printer is set to "print to scale" or to "full size" to make sure they come out the right size for your other materials!

- Use a cutting mat, or similar surface, for cutting lengths of craft sticks, skewers, and anything else you may need.

- Use the sharp end of a pencil to make small holes in cardboard (see page 7 for method) or ask an adult to help, using either scissors or a craft knife.

- Ask an adult to help straighten out and shape paper clips using a pair of pliers.

- Where strong glue is required, you may want to use a glue gun. Make sure you ask permission, and do not use it without an adult present. Strong liquid glue, such as wood or epoxy glue, will work well, too.

★ EASY

★★ MEDIUM

★★★ HARDER

You will find stars in the corner of the first page of each craft. These stars are a guide to the difficulty level of each project. They show you when you may need another pair of hands!

SAFETY FIRST!

Be careful and use good sense when making these models. They are easy to understand but will require some cutting, gluing, drilling, and other awkward tasks that you may need some help with from an adult.

WHEN TO GET HELP

Watch out for this sign throughout the book. You may need help from an adult when completing these tasks.

DISCLAIMER

The author, publisher, and bookseller cannot take responsibility for your safety. When you make and try out the projects, you do so at your own risk. Look out for the safety warning symbol (shown above) given throughout the book and call on adult assistance when you are cutting materials or using a pair of scissors or pliers, craft drill, or hot glue.

SAFETY FIRST!

HOW TO SCORE PAPER OR CARD SAFELY:

Using a ruler as a guide, press along the line with a hard plastic item, like the end of a pen lid. Do this on a cutting mat to protect the surface you're working on.

HOW TO MAKE HOLES IN CARDBOARD SAFELY AND EASILY:

Pressing a pencil point through cardboard and into an eraser, like the photo on the right, is a safe and easy way to make holes.

SPECTACULAR MODEL SPACECRAFT

Humans have been curious about outer space for centuries, but it wasn't until the 1950s that the first spacecraft went beyond **Earth's atmosphere.**

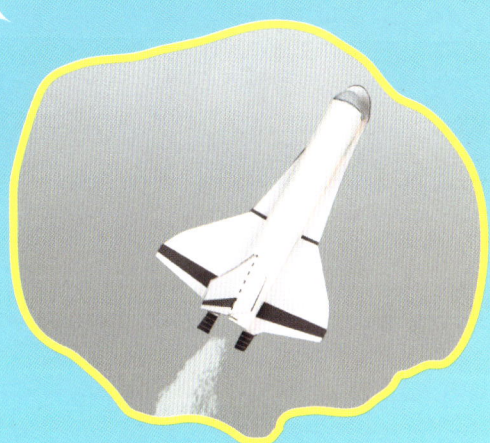

PREPARING FOR LIFTOFF
Spacecraft, like rockets, need to be strong and super fast to escape the pull of Earth's **gravity**. Because everything is so far away in space travel, spacecraft also need to carry lots of heavy fuel. This can make flying more difficult.

SPACECRAFT EXPLORATION
Scientists have learned more about outer space by sending clever robotic machines to explore where humans haven't yet been. Rovers on Mars are controlled by **NASA**'s scientists on Earth. It takes about 7 months to get them there, and not all rovers have landed safely!

WANT TO KNOW MORE?
This book allows you to make your very own model spacecraft. They may be smaller than real-life rockets, shuttles, and planet-exploring machines, but they can still fly, hover, and zoom!

STOMP ROCKET

5... 4... 3... 2... 1... LIFTOFF!
How high can you catapult your rocket with this out-of-this-world project?

Use the QR code to access the template you need.

WHAT YOU NEED:
- Thin plain paper
- Assorted card
- Corrugated cardboard
- Paper straw 6mm
- Paper straw 8mm
- Felt-tip pens or pencils

TOOLS:
- Pencil
- Ruler
- Pair of scissors
- Strong craft glue

KEY WORD
BELLOWS

A bellows is something that blows air through a tube or small opening in order to make something else work. In this project, the bellows pushes air through the straw to make the rocket fly!

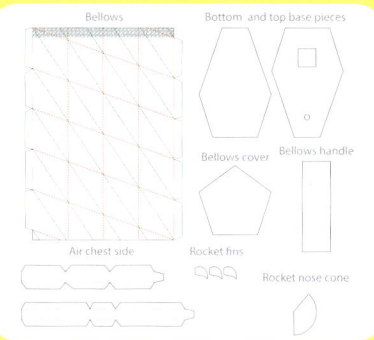

1 Print, copy, or trace the shapes from the template onto the specified materials and cut out.

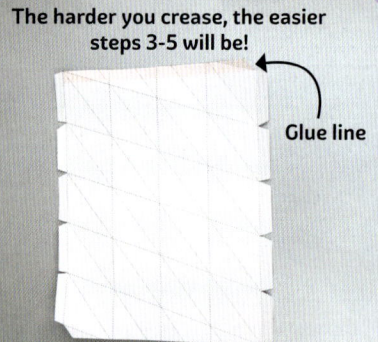

The harder you crease, the easier steps 3-5 will be!
Glue line

2 To make the bellows, score along the dotted and dashed lines (see page 7). Fold to crease all the lines and reopen the paper.

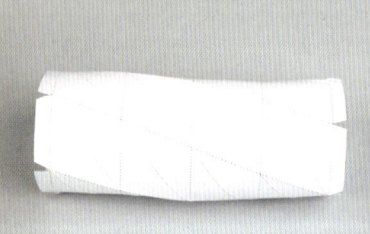

3 Flip the paper over, keeping the glue line at the top. Roll up from the bottom to make a tube. Line up the edges carefully, then glue along the glue line.

4 Starting from one end, fold in the sections. Use the red and green codes on the template to help guide you. Fold down on the green dotted lines (valley folds) and fold up on the red dashed lines (hill folds). **Scan the QR code above to watch how to fold the bellows.**

5 Work your way down the tube, folding one section at a time. The completed bellows should look like the image above.

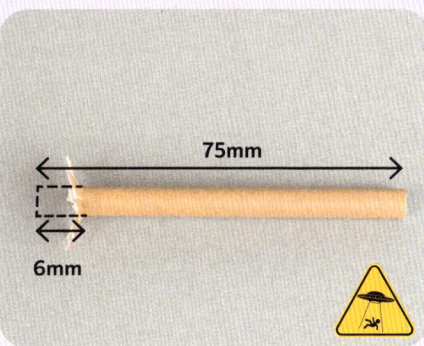

6 Cut the thin straw to 75mm. Cut glue strips at one end of the straw 6mm deep and bend outward.

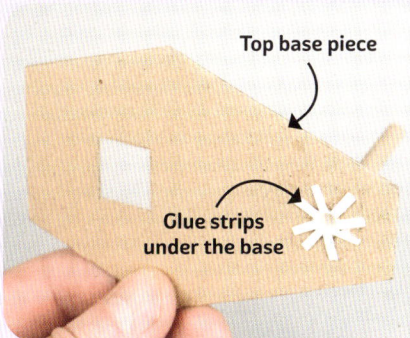

7 Thread the straw into the circular hole in the top base piece as shown. Glue the strips to stick them to the underneath.

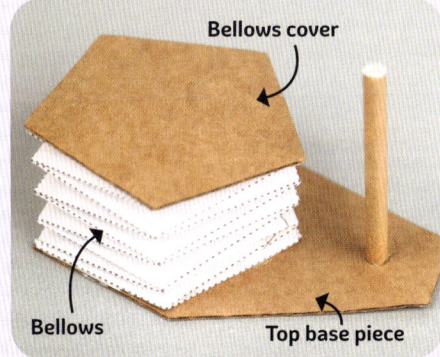

8 Glue the bellows to the top of the top base piece, lining up the bottom edge. Then, glue the bellows cover from the template on top.

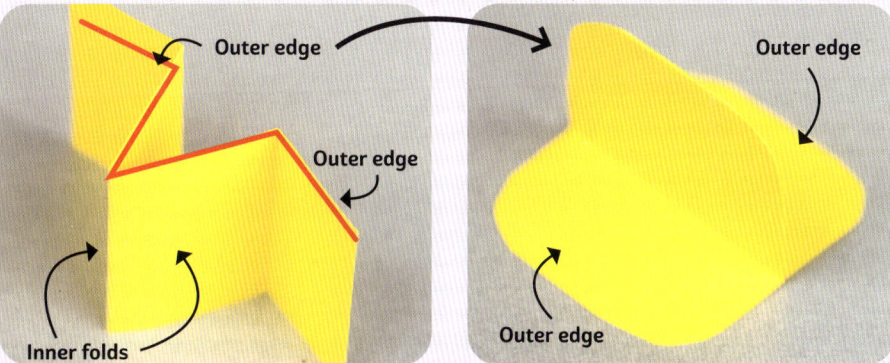

9 Take the bellows handle from the template. Fold along the dotted and dashes lines to crease the zigzag shape shown. Glue the inner folds together, leaving the outer edges folded outward. Cut the corners to make them rounded as shown.

10 Glue the handle to the top of the bellows cover. Then, set aside until step 12.

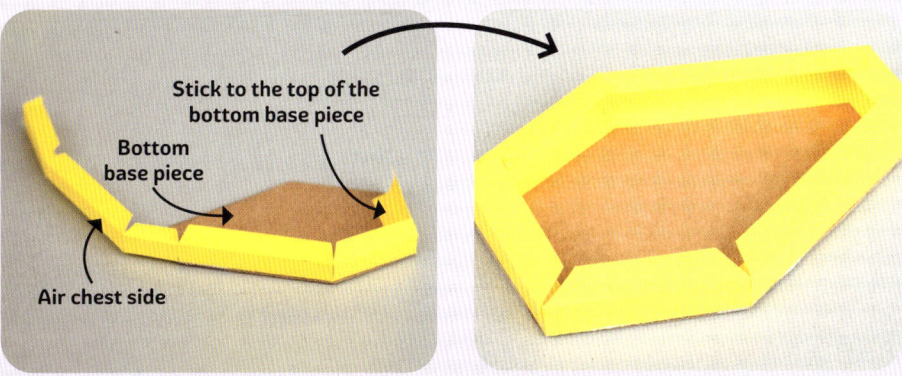

11 Using the letter guides on the template, wrap and glue the air chest side pieces around the bottom base piece. It should fit all the way around and look like the photo above.

Top base piece

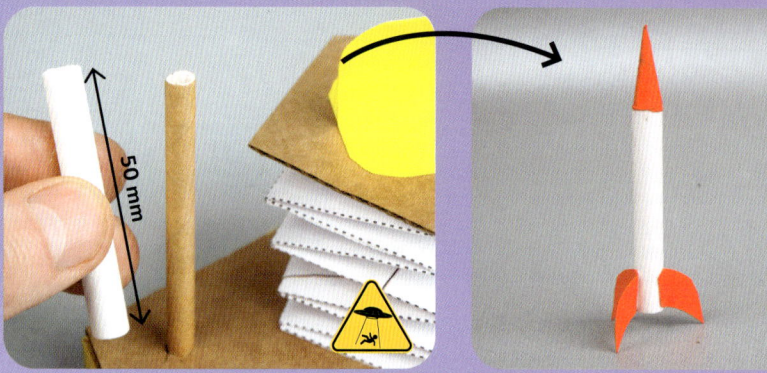

50 mm

12 Apply glue to the top of the air chest side, line up the top base piece on top and press down to glue together.

13 To make your rocket, cut the wider straw to 50mm in length so it's slightly shorter than the straw in the top base piece. Add a paper cone to the top and fins to the bottom to decorate the rocket.

DID YOU KNOW?
Rockets must travel faster than 7 miles per second to escape Earth's gravity – the force pulling them back to the ground. This speed is called **escape velocity**. It takes lots of fuel and power to travel that fast!

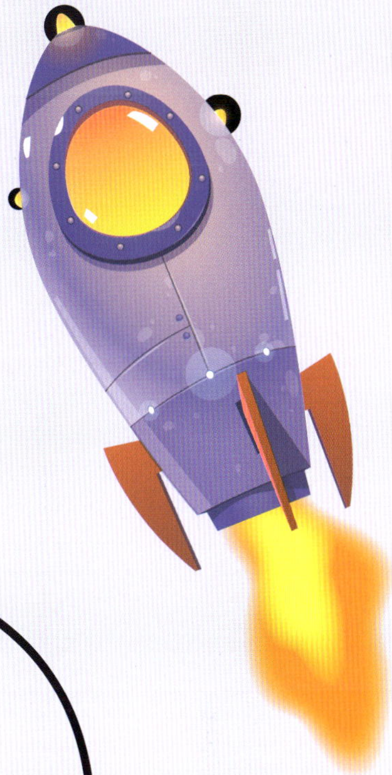

PRESS DOWN THE BELLOWS SHARPLY TO LAUNCH THE ROCKET INTO SPACE!

MOON LANDER

Make a simple Moon lander model with this clever craft. What do you think it's like to land on the Moon?

WHAT YOU NEED:
- Electrical connector block
- Long split pins

TOOLS:
- Strong craft glue
- Needle pliers
- Screwdriver

1 Carefully cut out four of the brass sections from the electrical connector block strip.

2 Glue the four connector blocks together with strong craft glue to make the body of the lander, as shown.

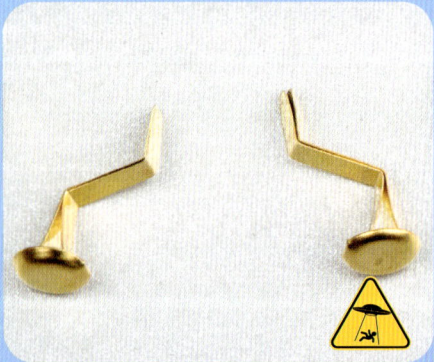

3 Ask an adult to bend angles into the split pins to make four legs.

4 Thread the legs into the brass blocks. Tighten the screws with a screwdriver to secure the legs in place.

CREATE A SPACE SCENE FOR YOUR AWESOME MOON LANDER!

DID YOU KNOW?
There's no wind on the Moon, which means that the first astronauts' footsteps are probably still there!

ROCKET CAROUSEL

Make a fantastic fairground carousel featuring rocket rides!

 | **Use the QR code to access the template you need.** | **WHAT YOU NEED:**
• Assorted card
• Corrugated cardboard
• Wooden skewer, cut to 75mm | **TOOLS:**
• Pencil
• Pair of scissors
• Strong craft glue |

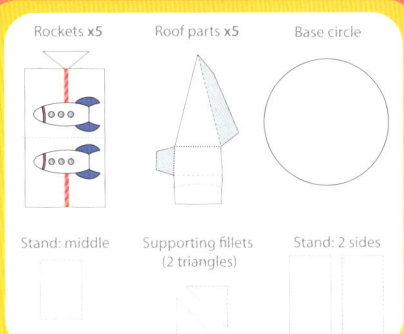

1 Print, copy, or trace the shapes from the template onto the specified materials and cut out.

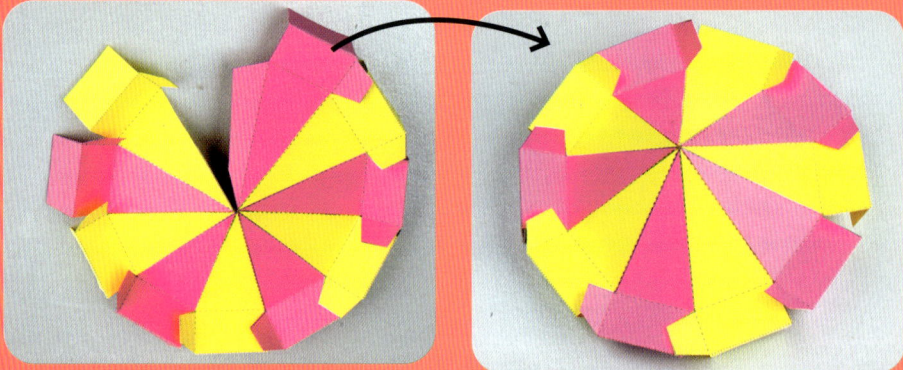

2 Crease and score (see page 7) along the fold lines of the roof parts from the template. Using alternating pieces, glue the main triangle sections together using the glue flaps as shown. Fitting in the final piece will make a shallow cone shape.

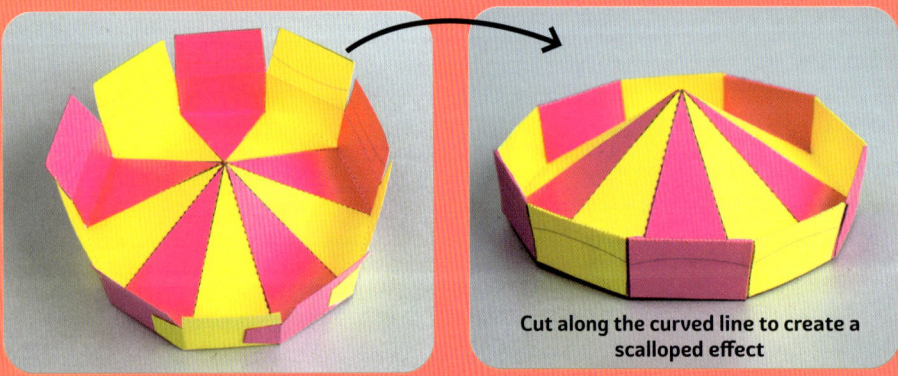

Cut along the curved line to create a scalloped effect

3 Fold up the outer edges to make them vertical. Then, layer and glue the outer edge pieces together using the glue tabs. Fold backward along the straight line of each outer piece and glue down to hide the glue tabs.

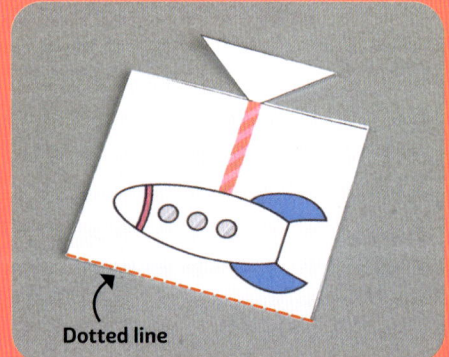

Dotted line

4 For the rockets, fold along the dotted line so that the pictures show on each side. They need to perfectly line up so they're double-sided once cut out.

5 Unfold, apply glue to the paper, and refold. Allow it to dry, then carefully cut out the rocket as shown. Repeat for all five rockets.

6 Turn the roof upside down, then glue the triangle section above the rockets to alternate sections of the roof.

7 To make the stand, place the smaller cardboard piece between the two bigger pieces. Line up the bottoms and glue together.

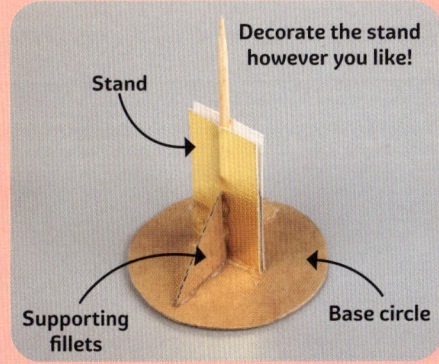

8 Glue the stand upright in the middle of the base circle, followed by one supporting fillet on each side. Glue and slide the skewer into the middle.

GIVE YOUR CAROUSEL A PUSH TO SET THE ROCKETS SPINNING!

MARS ROVER

Make an amazing Mars rover which can zoom around at super speed!

Use the QR code to access the template you need.

WHAT YOU NEED:
- 8 milk bottle tops
- Thick, shiny card
- Corrugated cardboard
- Long, thin rubber band
- 2 wooden skewers, cut to 80mm each

TOOLS:
- Pencil and eraser
- Pair of scissors
- Strong craft glue
- Small craft drill

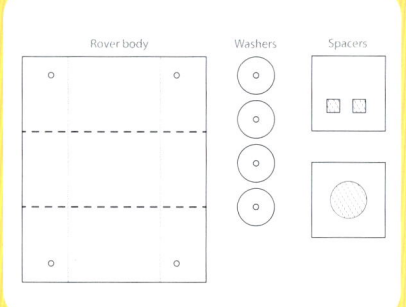

1 Print, copy, or trace the shapes from the template onto the specified materials and cut out.

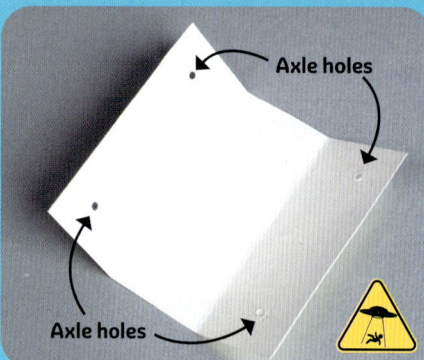

2 Make the axle holes (see page 7) on the rover's body, where specified on the template. Crease along the fold lines.

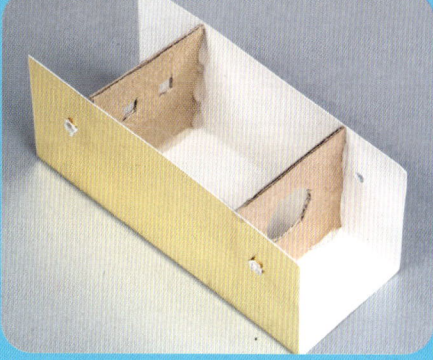

3 Stand the spacers on the lines indicated on the template. Glue the three edges touching the rover body to secure them.

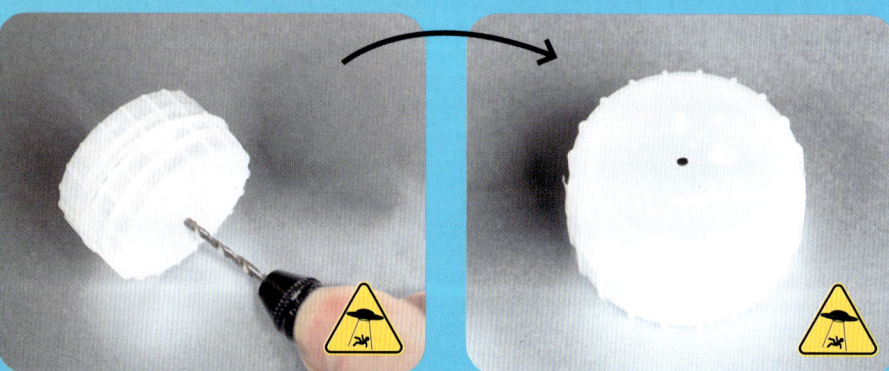

4 Ask an adult to make holes in the middle of each milk bottle top using a small craft drill. The holes must be precise for the craft to work. Test the holes are lined up by threading a skewer through. Once happy, split the tops into pairs, gluing each pair together along their bottom edges.

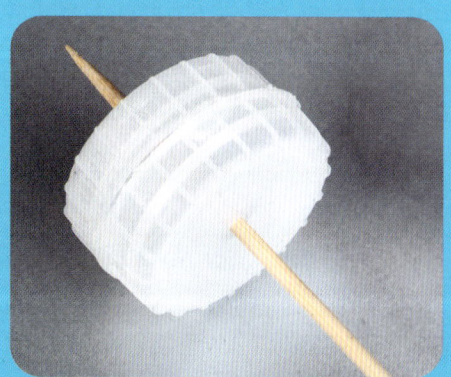

5 Once dry, thread a wooden skewer through one wheel and glue around the holes to attach.

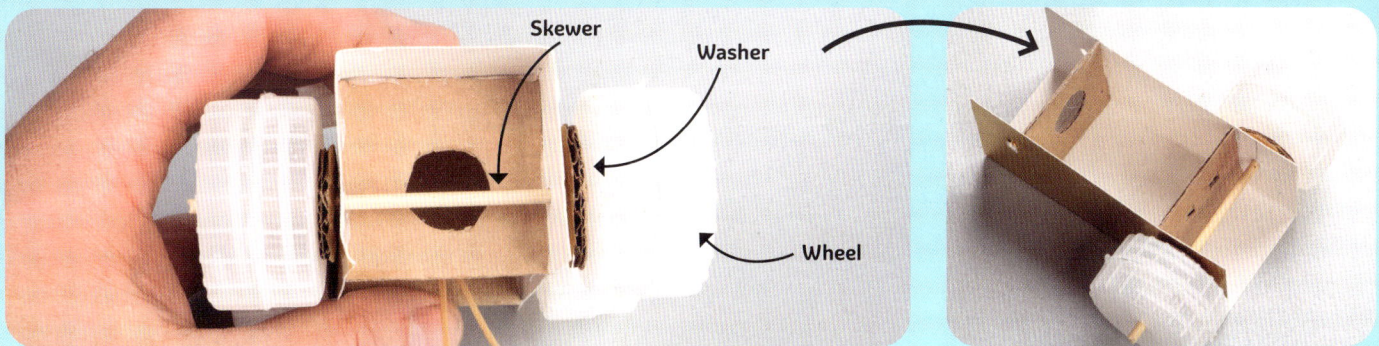

6 Thread a cardboard washer onto the skewer, pushing it up to the wheel. Thread the skewer through a pair of axle holes, sandwiching the washer between the wheel and the rover body. Slide a washer and wheel onto the other side of the skewer. Trim the skewer, leaving a little at each side, and glue the wheel in place. Repeat for the second set of wheels.

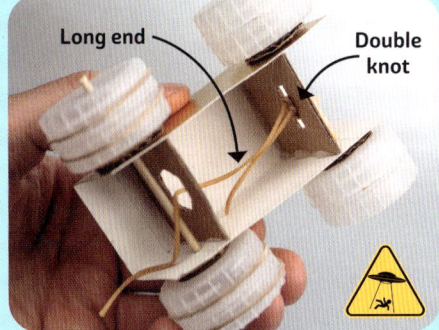

7 Cut a rubber band to make a single length. Tie it in a double knot through the double-holed spacer, leaving one side very long.

8 To use the rover, wrap the long end of the rubber band around the opposite skewer and wind up until tight. Place the rover on a flat surface, then release!

TOP TIP

If you get too much wheel spin, you can increase the grip by adding short rubber bands around the wheels (see steps 7 and 8).

WATCH THE THE ROVER DASH ALONG!

BLOWPIPE SPACE SHUTTLE

Launch your very own space shuttle with this quick, cool craft!

Use the QR code to access the template you need.

WHAT YOU NEED:
- Paper straw 6mm
- Paper straw 8mm
- Sticky putty
- Plain paper

TOOLS:
- Pair of scissors
- Strong craft glue
- Ruler

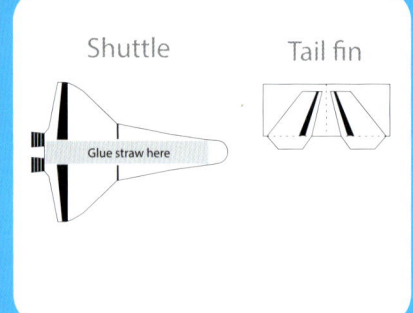

1 Print, copy, or trace the shapes from the template onto plain paper and cut out.

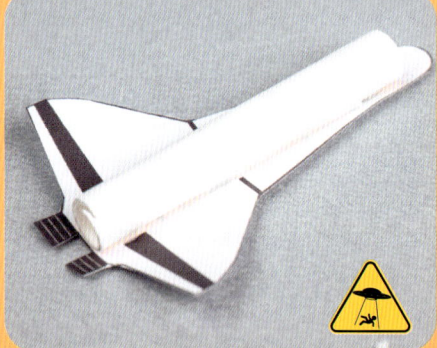

2 Cut the 8mm wide straw to 55mm long. Place the straw on top of the shuttle and glue in place.

3 Fold the wings up slightly as shown. The angle of the wings is called dihedral. It helps with stability in flight.

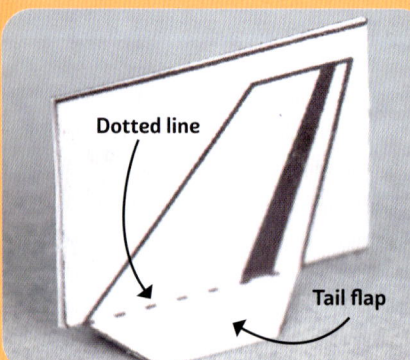

4 Fold the tail fin piece in half along the dotted line. Glue these two sides together, but don't glue the tail flaps.

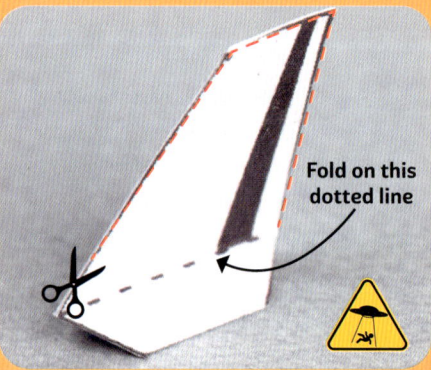

5 Cut around the tail fin as shown. Fold along the dotted lines of the tail flaps and open them outward.

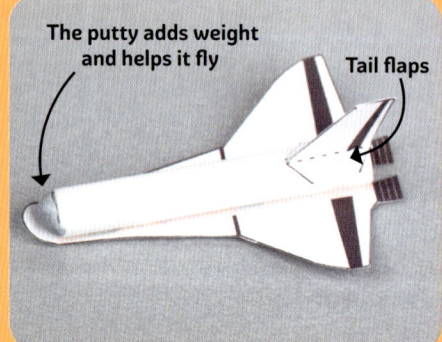

6 Glue the tail flaps to the straw as shown. Place a small piece of sticky putty on the other end of the straw.

7 Thread your shuttle onto the 6mm straw. Launch the shuttle by blowing a sharp breath through the straw.

5... 4... 3... 2... 1... BLAST OFF!

DID YOU KNOW?
The NASA space shuttle was the first spacecraft that could be used again and again. Each time a space shuttle was launched, it was called a mission. The space shuttle went on 135 missions in total!

ORIGAMI MARS LANDER

TOP TIP

Origami is a lot easier to follow when watching a video! Scan the QR code to watch how to make it.

Use the QR code to see a video of the steps in action.

Origami, the Japanese art of folding paper into decorative shapes and figures, is a fun way to make models!

WHAT YOU NEED:
- Origami paper 150 x 150mm square

1 Start with a single square sheet of paper with the diagonals, vertical and horizontal lines creased.

2 Fold from the top right corner to the bottom left. Then, tuck in the other two corners to make a smaller square. Rotate the square 45 degrees so that the open end is at the bottom.

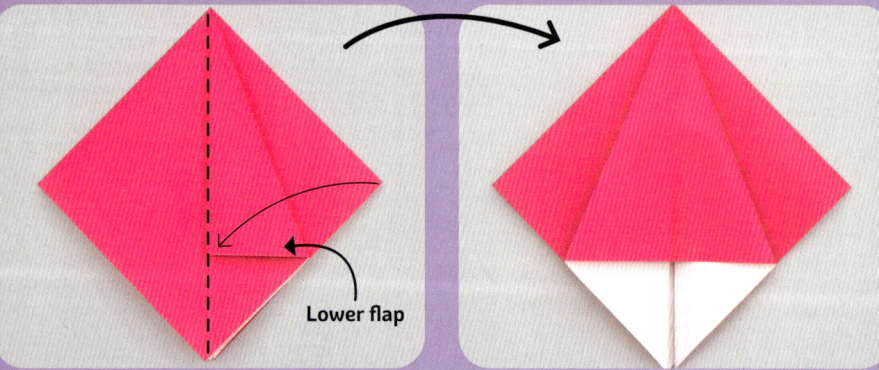

3 Fold in the right corner to the middle line to create a crease. Pull the lower flap out from underneath (by inserting your fingers under the folded area). Open out and flatten the fold by pulling the flap to the bottom left edge to make an inverted kite shape. Crease the paper in place.

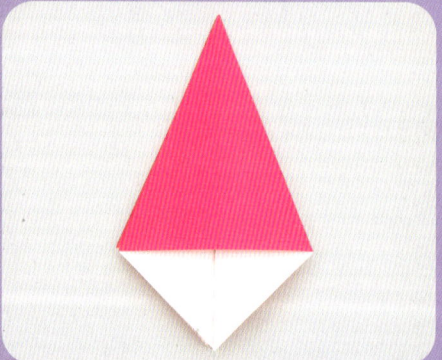

4 Flip the paper over and repeat step 3 three more times with the other flaps, like the above image.

 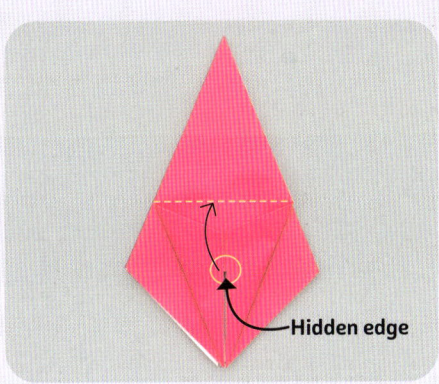 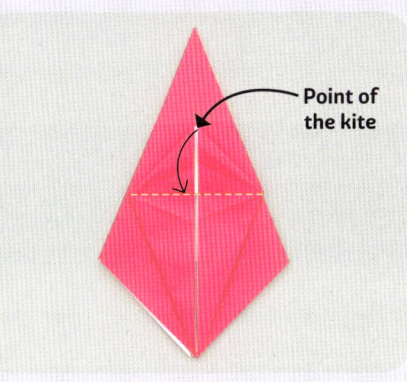

5 Fold in the left and right corners to the vertical middle line.

6 Pull up the hidden edge and fold it backward to the vertical middle line, making a kite shape.

7 Fold down the point of the kite. Repeat steps 5-6 three more times around the model.

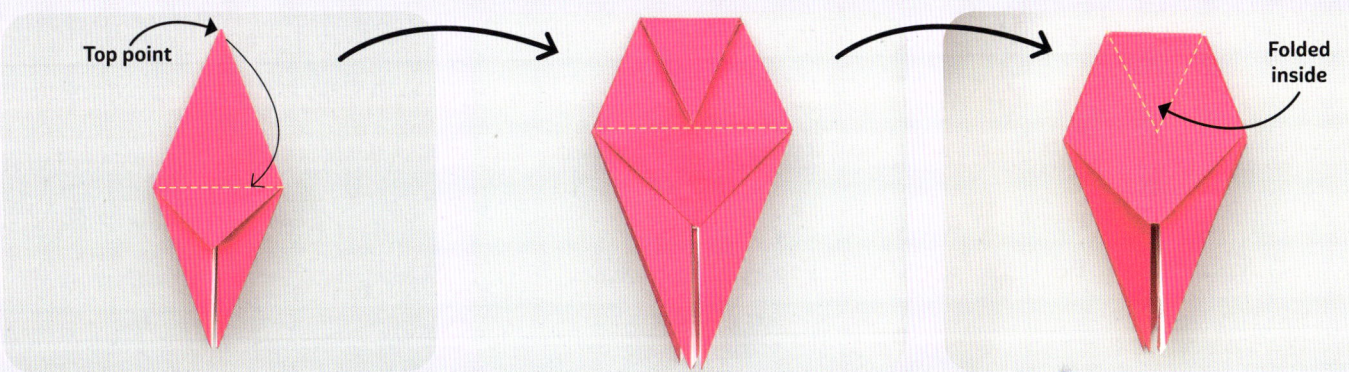

8 Fold down the top point to the horizontal line shown and push down to crease. Then, open the fold, flip the model over and repeat on the other side. Loosely open out the model, then push down the newly folded section into the top of the model so that it's tucked inside. Fold the model flat again.

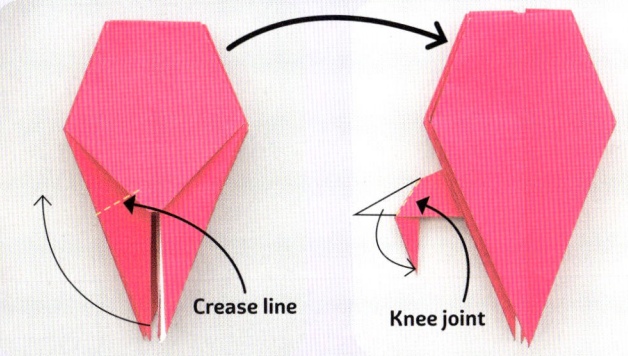 

9 Fold up a leg along the crease line as shown. Fold down the knee joint of the leg. Then, repeat this step for the remaining three legs before opening out the model to complete your Mars lander.

BALANCING UFO

This spaceship hovers mysteriously off the ground. Which faraway planet or **galaxy** do think it has come from?

Use the QR code to access the template you need.

WHAT YOU NEED:
- Assorted card
- Corrugated cardboard circle
- Table tennis ball
- Craft cork
- Split pins
- Jumbo paper clip
- Bouncy rubber ball 25mm
- Lollipop stick or paper straw

TOOLS:
- Pencil
- Ruler
- Pair of scissors
- Strong craft glue
- Pointy wooden skewer
- Needle pliers
- Sticky tape
- Marker pen

1 Print, copy, or trace the shapes from the template onto the specified materials and cut out.

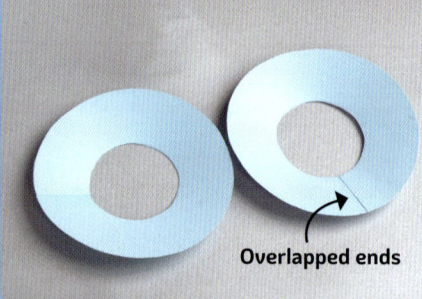

2 Take one saucer ring, overlap the ends, and glue them down. This should create a dome shape. Repeat with the other ring.

3 Place the rings over the table tennis ball with the dome sides facing outward. Glue the edges down to keep the ball secure.

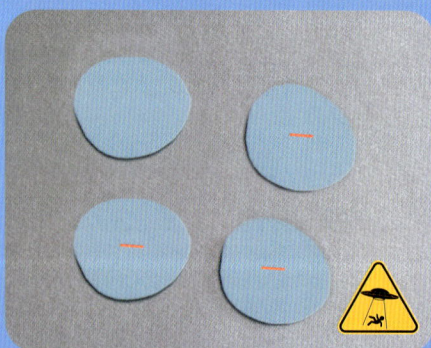

4 To make the legs, cut a small slit in the middle of three of the card circles from the template.

5 Thread a split pin through the slits and bend the tips in opposite directions. Repeat for the other legs.

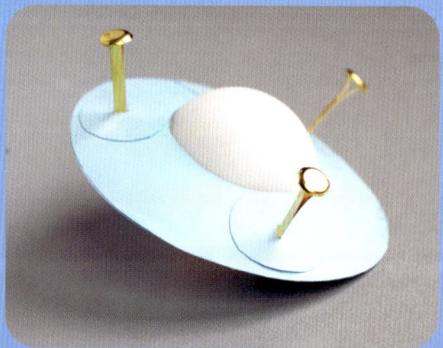

6 Attach the legs to the saucer by gluing the circle ends to the saucer ring. Make sure to space the legs evenly around.

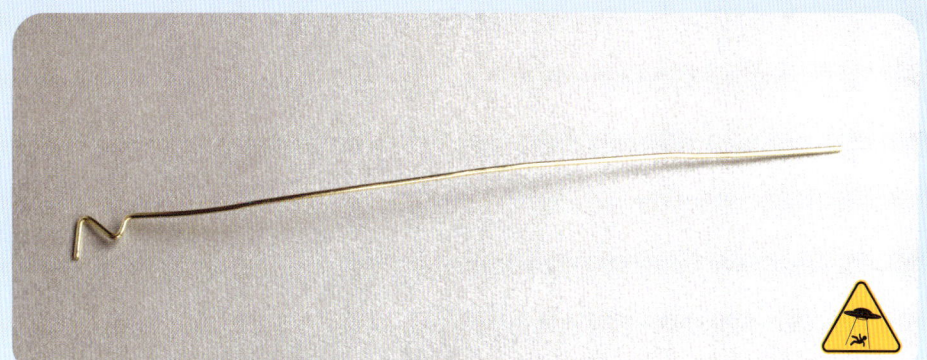
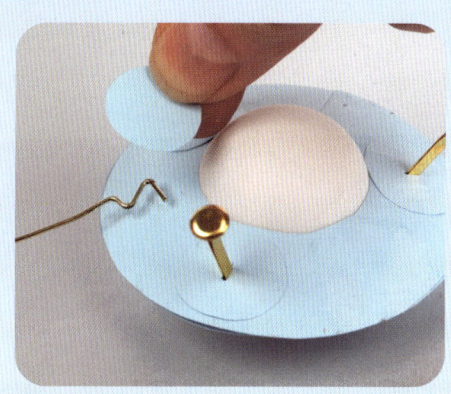

7 Ask an adult to use pliers to straighten out a jumbo paper clip, and add a zigzag to the end. This shape will be easier to attach to the UFO than a straight shape. If the paper clip is difficult to bend, you could use thick craft wire instead.

8 Attach the zigzag to the underside of the saucer using sticky tape. Glue the last circle on top to hide it.

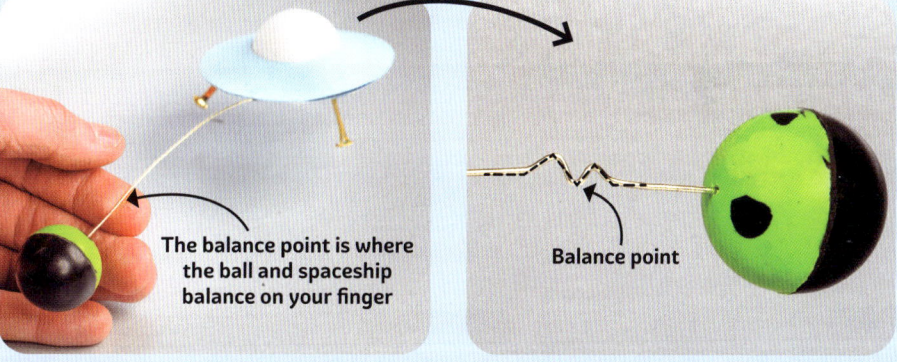

9 Pierce the bouncy ball with the other end of the paper clip to make a small hole, then push it in firmly.

10 Run your finger along the wire to find the place where the spaceship and bouncy ball are equally balanced. Mark this place (called the balance point) with a marker pen. Fold an M shape into the wire at the balance point.

11 Dig out a small hole 13mm deep into the top of the cork, using a pointy skewer. The hole needs to be wide enough for a lollipop stick or paper straw to fit inside. Glue the cork to the middle of a circle of corrugated cardboard. The circle can be any size, this is just a base for the UFO.

12 Carefully cut a 25mm length from a lollipop stick or strong paper straw and fit it into the hole in the cork.

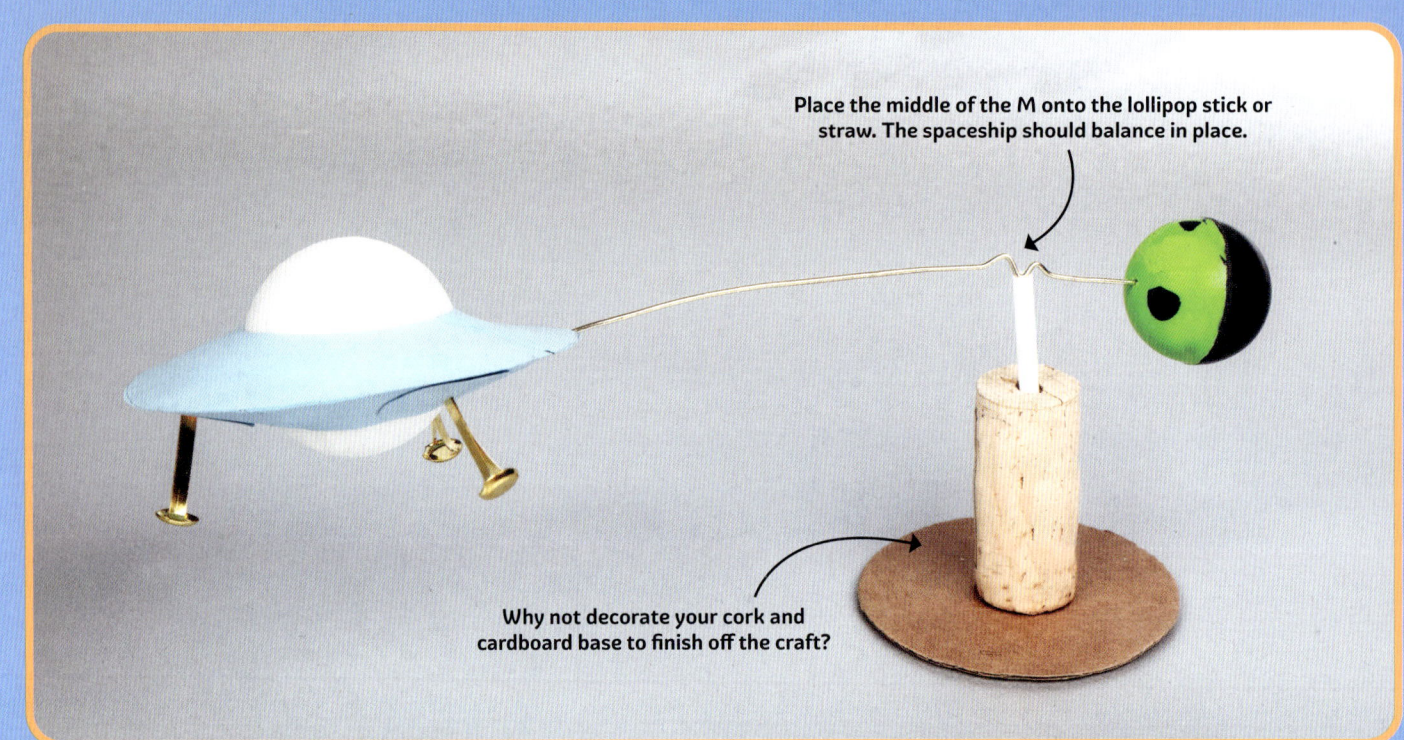

Place the middle of the M onto the lollipop stick or straw. The spaceship should balance in place.

Why not decorate your cork and cardboard base to finish off the craft?

WATCH THE UFO HOVER MYSTERIOUSLY!

DID YOU KNOW?
UFO stands for Unidentified Flying Object. This can be anything in the sky that the person who saw it can't explain. Some people claim to have seen UFOs that look like alien spaceships, but no scientific evidence has been found to confirm alien life… yet!

DID YOU KNOW?
Scientists believe that for another planet to have **intelligent life** on it, it must be similar to Earth in a few ways. It probably needs an atmosphere (air), water, and light and heat caused by **orbiting** a star (like the Sun).

AMAZING SPACECRAFT

As we've seen, spacecraft can come in different shapes and sizes depending on the jobs they're built to do, but how do these amazing machines work? Let's discover the secrets behind super spacecraft.

X-15 ROCKET PLANE
This experimental, superfast rocket-powered aircraft first flew in 1959. It was the first manned aircraft to reach the edge of space and the world's first piloted aircraft to reach **hypersonic** speeds. It reached 4,520 miles per hour – that's more than 5 times the speed of sound! It helped scientists and engineers build future spacecraft.

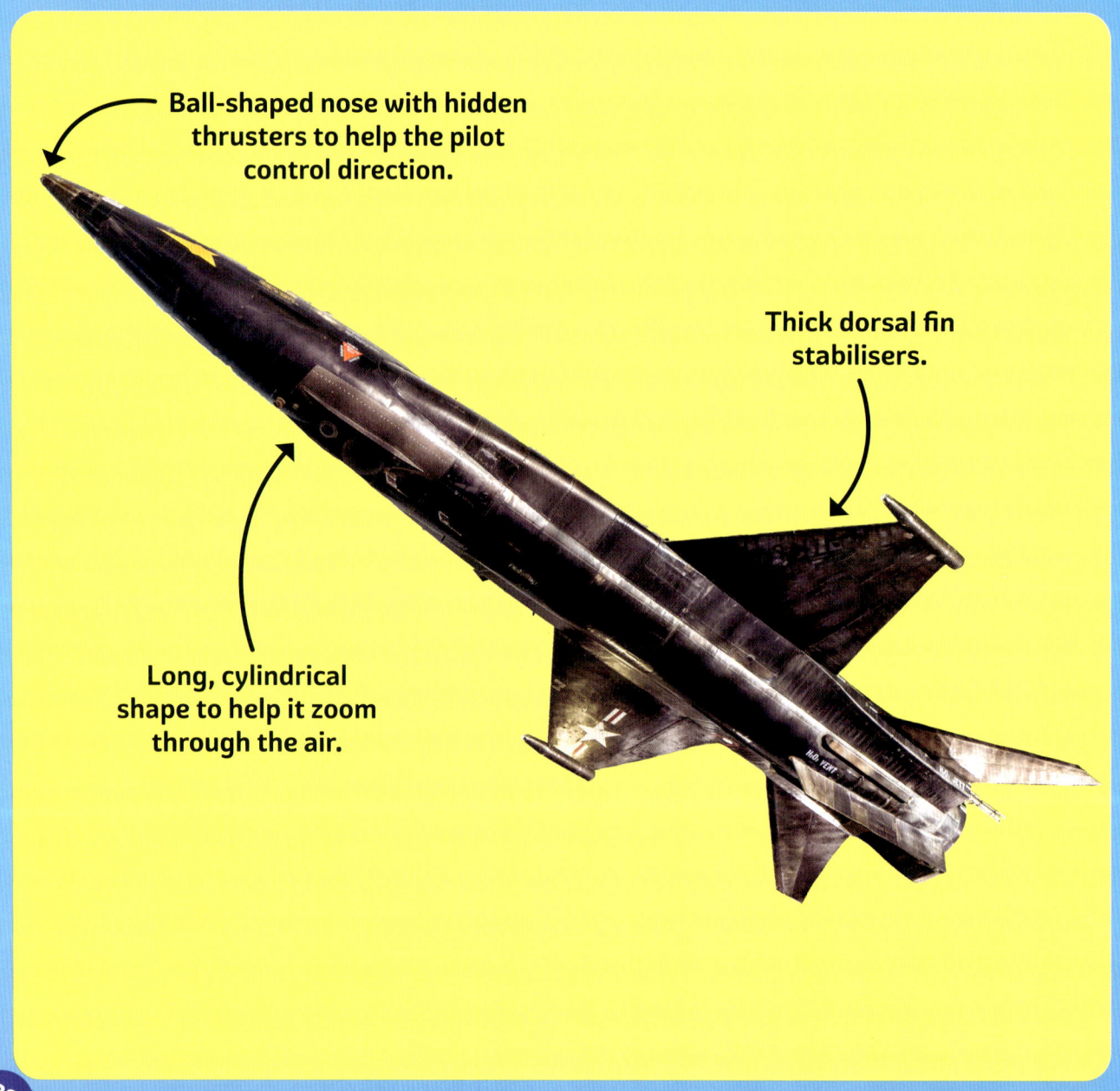

Ball-shaped nose with hidden thrusters to help the pilot control direction.

Thick dorsal fin stabilisers.

Long, cylindrical shape to help it zoom through the air.

SUPER SPACE SHUTTLE

The space shuttle was the only manned winged aircraft that could move in and out of orbit, returning its crew and cargo. Its robotic arm was used to fix the **International Space Station** and carry out repairs on the **Hubble Space Telescope**. To escape gravity and reach orbit, the shuttle had to accelerate from 0 to 8,000m per second (almost 18,000 miles per hour) in 8 and a half minutes!

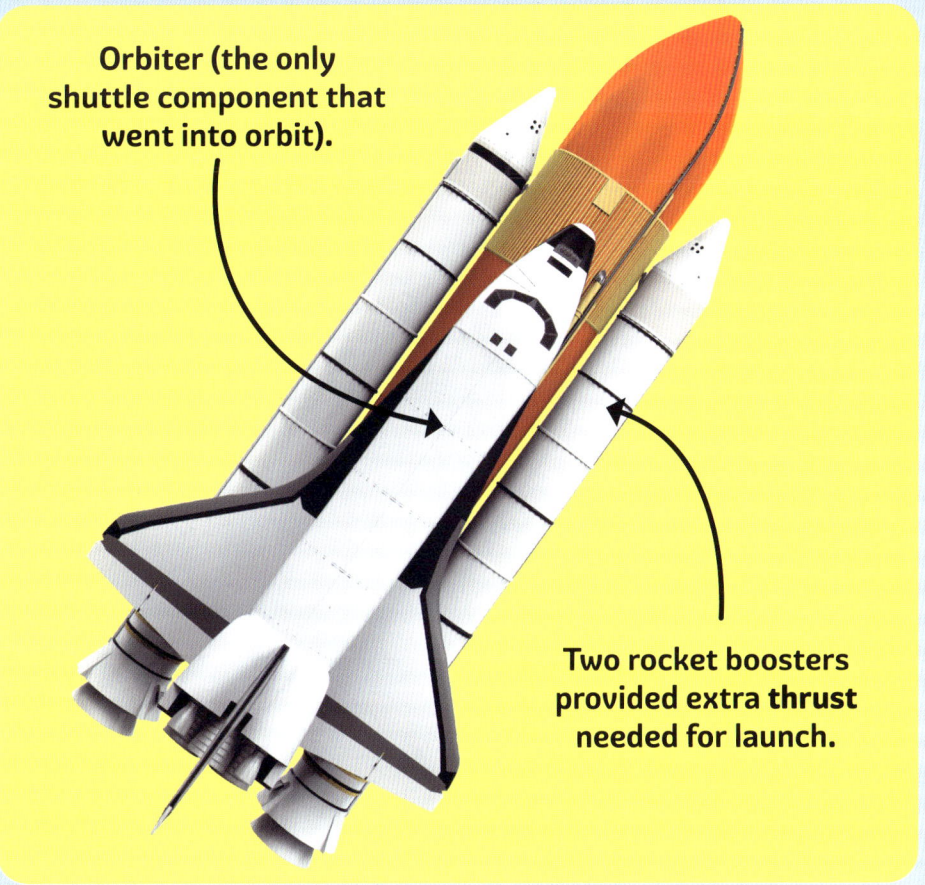

Orbiter (the only shuttle component that went into orbit).

Two rocket boosters provided extra **thrust** needed for launch.

EXPLORING LANDERS

Spacecraft designed to land on other planets have extra features that aren't needed on flight-only vehicles. Apollo 11, the spacecraft used in the 1969 Moon landing, was made of two main parts: the command module, where the pilot stayed, orbiting the Moon; and the lunar module, which detached and landed on the Moon.

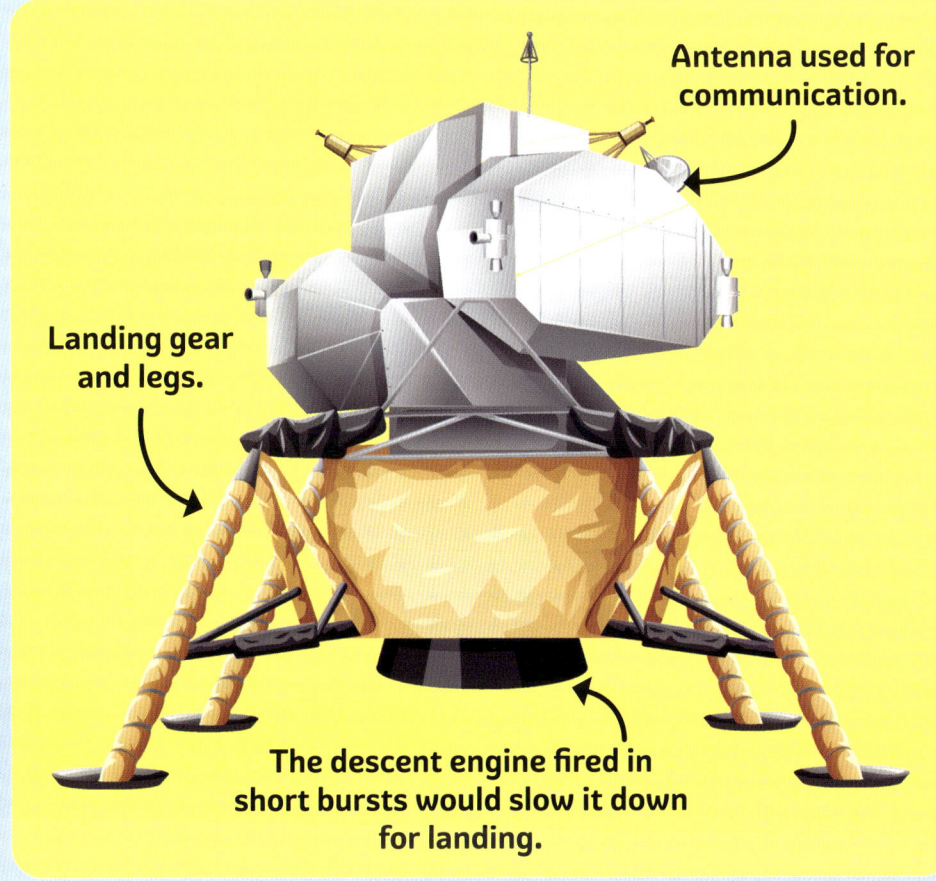

Antenna used for communication.

Landing gear and legs.

The descent engine fired in short bursts would slow it down for landing.

PREPARING FOR LAUNCH

It's not easy to design and build a spacecraft, but it takes even more planning and coordination to launch it into space. It takes lots of people, all experts in their jobs, to create a successful mission.

AMAZING ASTRONAUTS
These are the scientists and engineers who travel into outer space, and are trained to work inside and outside spacecraft. Training can take many years: astronauts must be very fit, strong, and brave to cope with going into, and being in, space.

EXCELLENT ENGINEERS
There are lots of different types of engineers who work on spacecraft from building to preparing for launch. Some of the most important are the payload engineers who make sure that spacecraft and **satellites** have all the technology they need to communicate with scientists on Earth, and to complete their mission objectives.

MISSION CONTROL

Spacecraft launches and missions are supervised from mission control, which is a huge room filled with computers and expert scientists and engineers. These people all have different jobs but work together as one big team to monitor the spacecraft and astronauts through their journey to space, from takeoff to landing back on Earth.

Guidance officer helps with spacecraft navigation.

The flight director is in charge of updating leaders with how the mission is going.

Flight control team work on data from the spacecraft and launch systems.

PREPARED FOR EVERYTHING

Every mission is different, and there are lots of dangers with space flight. Mission control workers go through drills and simulations to test their reactions, and make sure they're prepared to help astronauts with any tricky situation that could come up!

GLOSSARY

Earth's atmosphere - layers of gases surrounding Earth which are held in place by gravity (see right).

Escape velocity - the constant velocity (speed and direction) needed for an object to escape from a planet's gravitational pull.

Galaxy - a huge collection of gas, dust, and billions of stars and their solar systems, all held together by gravity (see right).

Gravity - a pulling force that works across space. Objects don't have to touch each other for gravity to affect them. For example, the Sun, which is millions of miles away, pulls on Earth and the other planets and objects in the solar system to keep them in orbit.

Hubble Space Telescope - an incredibly big and strong telescope which orbits Earth and sends back amazing photos of outer space.

Hypersonic - something which moves five or more times faster than the speed of sound.

Intelligent life - living beings in the universe that can think, learn and understand things like humans.

International Space Station (ISS) - a large spacecraft in Earth's orbit which is used as a base for scientific research.

NASA - the National Aeronautics and Space Administration is an agency that deals with space research and exploration. They're based in the USA.

Orbit – the repeated path taken by one object circling around another object in space.

Satellite - any object that orbits a planet. Satellites can be natural, like moons, or artificial (man-made items), like the communications satellites we use to send phone calls and TV signals, and for weather forecasting!

Thrust - the force that pushes something in a particular direction. For example, the power of a rocket's engine pushes the spacecraft forward.

INDEX

A
aliens 26
astronauts 15, 30,31
atmosphere 8, 27, 29

E
Earth 8-9, 12, 27, 30-31
engineers 28-29, 30-31

G
gravity 9, 12, 29, 32

H
Hubble Space Telescope 29, 32

I
International Space Station 29, 32

L
landers 14-15, 22-23, 29

M
Mars 9, 18-19, 22-23
Moon 14-15, 29

R
rockets 9, 10-11, 12-13, 16-17, 28
rovers 9, 18-19

S
shuttle 9, 20-21, 29
spacecraft 8-9, 10-11, 12-13, 14-15, 16-17, 18-19, 20-21, 28-29, 30-31
Sun 27

U
UFO 24-25, 26-27

PICTURE CREDITS:

(Abbreviations: t=top, b=bottom, m=middle, l=left, r=right, bg=background)

Shutterstock: BlueRingMedia 29bl; Digital Images Studio 14-15b; Dima Zel 21b; Erik Cox Photography 28m; FishCoolish Astronaut character throughout; Frame Stock Footage 30tr; Helen Dream 8b; Klyaksun spaceship/rocket throughout; Nerthuz 29tr; Paulista 26-27bg; SAVE MEDIA CONTENT 31m; Sergey Nivens 12b. NASA Images: 2-3b; NASA/Frank Michaux 30bl.

Every effort has been made to trace the copyright holders, and we apologise in advance for any unintentional omissions. We would be pleased to insert the appropriate acknowledgements in any subsequent edition of this publication.